Cruelty to Animals

ADAM HIBBERT

WITHDRAWN
FROM STOCK

FRANKLIN WATTS
LONDON•SYDNEY

First published in 2005 by Franklin Watts
96 Leonard Street, London EC2A 4XD

Franklin Watts Australia
Level 17/207 Kent Street
Sydney NSW 2000

Copyright © Franklin Watts 2005

Series editor: Rachel Cooke
Series design: White Design
Picture research: Diana Morris

Dewey Classification: 179'.3
A CIP catalogue record for this book is available from the British Library.

ISBN: 0 7496 6299 9

Printed in China

Acknowledgements:
Get the Facts Straight, page 4, Food & Agriculture Organization (FAO), UN;
Get the Facts Straight page 11 AARDAS & pet-abuse.com; Get the Facts Straight, page 19, Doris Hofer,
The Lion's Share of the Hunt, TRAFFIC Europe regional report (2002); Get the Facts Straight, page 23,
www.biosecurity.govt.nz and www.rds-online.org.uk

Photographic credits: Associated Press: 21bl. Jeff Chagrin/Rex Features: 10. Bob Daemmrich/Image
Works/Topham: 24. Robert Dowling/Corbis: 16bl. Angela Hampton/RSPCA Photo Library: 8. Martin
Harvey/Still Pictures: 21tr. Philippe Hays/Still Pictures: 15t, 18, 20. Peter Hvizdak/Image
Works/Topham: 19. Steve Jones/Ecoscene: 17. Kladderadatsch, 1933: 26t. Luiz C. Marigo/Still
Pictures: 9. Thomas Nykrog/Scanpix: 26b. Pete Oxford/RSPCA Photo Library: 7. Joe Partridge/Rex
Features: 27. Reuters/Corbis: 28. Rex Features: 25. RSPCA Photo Library: front cover, 6, 11, 14, 16tr.
Safehaven4donkeys.org: 13. Harmut Schwarzbach/Still Pictures: 12. Jorgen Schytte/Still Pictures: 4.
Sipa/Rex Features: 5, 22. Ray Tang/Rex Features: 29. Voisin/Phanie/Rex Features: 23.
Adam Woolfitt/Corbis: 15b.

CONTENTS

THE USE OF ANIMALS

HUMANS HAVE LONG relied on other animals for needs as far apart as food and friendship. This relationship has caused strong emotions in humans and issues linked to it often make headline news.

⬇ *For many, keeping livestock is essential for survival. A cow provides a poor family with milk to drink or sell, and with fertiliser for crops.*

ANIMALS FOR FOOD

Most people eat meat and, as the panel shows, global meat consumption is rising. Food animals have to be killed, but seeing such killing often upsets people. Industrial processes for killing animals seem especially heartless. The US animal activist group PeTA secretly filmed workers in a chicken slaughterhouse stamping on chickens. Although it promotes veganism, PeTA argues that gassing chickens is a more humane option.

ANIMALS FOR FRIENDSHIP

People often keep animals as companions, or pets. Pets normally enjoy much higher standards of care than any other animals. But they can be over-fed, and some animals are not suited to being pets. In 2005, there was a worldwide media scare that Harry Potter fans were buying owls as pets. It turned out to be a false alarm.

French activists protest outside a KFC restaurant in Paris over the poor treatment of the chickens used in the restaurant chain's food.

ANIMALS FOR KNOWLEDGE

Many people believe that using animals to test the safety of consumer goods, such as make-up, is wrong. Some animals are harmed to help improve medical knowledge, to save or improve human lives. The most extreme protest occurs against these uses of animals, with some activists resorting to terrorist-like violence.

ANIMALS FOR RECREATION

Religious rules, traditional rituals and games, hunting and using animals in races can all cause animal suffering. Some people who accept the harming of animals for "necessary" reasons, such as food, feel that these cultural uses are not necessary. In the UK, demands for a ban on hunting foxes with hounds began in 1949, and came into effect in February 2005.

GET THE FACTS STRAIGHT

World Meat Market	2003	2004	2005
Production*			
Poultry meat	76.0	77.2	79.9
Pig meat	98.6	100.9	103.6
Bovine meat	61.4	62.2	63.0
Sheep & goat meat	12.3	12.6	12.9
Other meat	4.9	5.0	5.0
Total	**253.1**	**257.9**	**264.3**
Consumption**			
Poultry meat	12.1	12.1	12.6
Pig meat	15.7	15.9	16.3
Bovine meat	9.8	9.8	9.9
Sheep & goat meat	1.9	2.0	2.0
Other meat	0.8	0.8	0.8
Total	**40.3**	**40.6**	**41.6**

*(million tonnes)
**(kg/head)

HUMANS USED ANIMALS with no concern for their welfare for thousands of years. Religion was the first widespread influence on our relationship to animals. Religious rules began to change attitudes to animals around 2,500 BCE. In the 1800s, ideas about animal welfare were made into laws. By the end of the 20th century, rights for animals became a more popular idea.

⬆ *This is a cartoon of an early court case brought by the animal welfare supporters against a man for cruelty to a donkey. The cartoonist is poking fun at both sides.*

RESPECT FOR ANIMALS

In the Indus valley civilization, around 4,500 years ago, animals appear to have been honoured or highly valued. In the Jain religion which arose around that time, animals are treated as having souls. Jains are vegans, refusing to eat animals. Jain monks sweep the ground as they walk, to avoid treading on small creatures.

ABRAHAMIC RELIGIONS

Judaism, Christianity and Islam come from one historical root, represented by Abraham. They share the attitude that animals are God's gift for humans to use. Judaism and Islam require believers to avoid pork, and to ensure food animals are killed according to religious rules. The Christian saint, Francis of Assisi (1181-1226) is said to have befriended animals.

HUMANE SOCIETIES

In the 1700s, the UK entered a modern, urban, industrial period. More people lived apart from farms and farm animals and began to think about animals in new ways. By 1822, the first laws were passed banning cruelty to horses and cattle. The Society for the Prevention of Cruelty to Animals was launched in 1824, to make sure the law was obeyed. It was given Royal approval in 1840 so it became known by the acronym RSPCA.

RIGHTS FOR ANIMALS

The humane societies did not oppose the use of animals, as long as they were treated with care. In the 1970s, a new movement emerged, aiming to free all animals from human use. It argued that animals have rights, but are "oppressed" by humans. This more radical approach to stopping cruelty was expressed in direct action, and, increasingly, in minor acts of terrorism.

➡ *For its attackers, bullfighting is deeply cruel. For its defenders, it is an art form with an ancient tradition.*

FACING THE ISSUES

Bullfighting has survived for over 2,000 years. It has roots in the "bull-leaping" rituals of ancient cultures such as the Minoans of Crete. The bull is weakened, and then killed by the matador, although a bull is sometimes spared if it performs well. The audience may side with either matador or bull. Ernest Hemingway, an American fan, said: "Bullfighting is the only art in which the artist is in danger of death." In newspapers in Spain, bullfighting is listed in the arts rather than sports pages. Now the art itself is threatened with death – a ban for cruelty to bulls.

UNINTENDED HARM

SOME ANIMALS SUFFER *as a result of human thoughtlessness, or due to accidents. Some animal welfare work focuses on informing and educating animal owners. In wealthier countries, this involves letting pet owners know about good practice. In less wealthy countries, it may involve helping farmers and hunters change how they live and work.*

⬆ *Small children need to learn how to handle a pet without hurting it.*

WHAT DO YOU THINK?

- Why do you think poverty can affect people's attitudes towards animals? Is need an excuse for cruelty?
- Do you think children should be taught how to look after animals in school? If so, what sort of things should they be taught?
- Accidents happen. Should anyone be held responsible for the harm done to animals as a result of an accident like an oil spill? What should be done to prevent such accidents?

HUMANE EDUCATION

Humane societies create leaflets, websites, and training courses to inform people how to care for animals. They also help politicians and others to set codes of conduct. In October 2004, for example, the Canadian Pork Council (CPC) sought advice from the Canadian Federation of Humane Societies. They helped the CPC to create new animal welfare tests for Canada's pig farmers.

MAKING A LIVING

Very poor people may exploit animals to earn a living, for example, by poaching rare animals. Some welfare groups pay for wardens to catch poachers. This sometimes leads to poachers being shot dead, as in Tsavo West National Park, Kenya, in January 2005. Creating alternative sources of income for poachers can be very difficult.

QUILLS AND SPILLS

Some accidents, such as oil tanker wrecks, can affect wild animals for hundreds of miles. Birds cannot clean off the oil, and sticky feathers leave them exposed to cold water and predators. So welfare experts collect them and shampoo the oil off. In 2003, the Prestige oil tanker sank in seas off northern Spain. Despite a massive rescue effort, around 300,000 birds were killed.

NATURAL DISASTER

If domesticated animals are left ownerless, they can go "feral" – reverting to a wild lifestyle. Welfare groups try to capture and sterilise feral animals, to keep their population levels low, aiding good health. In 2005, groups such as Humane Society International sent teams to the areas affected by the natural disaster of the tsunami in the Indian Ocean. They aimed to care for ownerless dogs and other animals.

⬇ *Despite people's efforts, many of the wild birds cleaned up after an oil spill will die as a result of the shock they suffer.*

DELIBERATE CRUELTY

SOME CRUELTY to animals is deliberate. Humans are sometimes cruel to the animals in their care, or to wild animals they catch, with no other goal than to make the animal suffer. This type of animal cruelty is rare, and most people oppose it. Cruelty may be a sign of mental disorder, fear or anger. Some welfare groups specialize in giving psychological help to animal torturers.

EARLY-WARNING SIGNAL?

Children with developmental problems are sometimes cruel to animals, deliberately torturing pets or wild animals. Many severely abnormal adults, such as serial killers, are known to have tortured animals when they were children. But "normal" people may also mistreat animals as they grow up – many will admit to having "played" with animals as a child, such as insects and frogs, before killing them.

ORGANIZED SADISM

Despite a ban under both Islamic law and state law, bears are "baited" in parts of rural Pakistan. They are declawed and detoothed, and then savaged by dogs, to entertain a paying crowd. In June 2001, the first bear to be saved from this treatment, nicknamed Rustam, was rehoused in Kund Park, a sanctuary in Northern Pakistan.

↙ *Bear baiting used to be a popular sport throughout Europe and Asia. It is now very rare.*

CRUELTY AS DEFENCE

People who work in abattoirs kill animals for a job. This can make it upsetting for them to think of the animals in their care with love or respect. A few cope by acting cruelly towards animals, treating them as objects or toys. This "defence mechanism" can go horribly wrong. In 2003, ex-abattoir worker John Bunting was convicted of 11 gruesome murders in Adelaide, Australia.

➔ *Mungo, one of three ponies rescued from a cruel owner, had hooves so overgrown that rescuers had to carry him to safety on a sheet.*

SADISTIC NEGLECT

Pets and companion animals such as dogs and ponies need space and care – for example, grooming – to stay healthy. Some owners deliberately ignore animals in their care, leaving them locked in sheds or stables. In June 2004, a man from Yorkshire, UK, was found to have severely neglected three ponies in his care. He was sent to prison for three months.

GET THE FACTS STRAIGHT

US Animal Abuse – Classifications
(Broken down from a sample of 3136 cases)

Classification	Number
Hanging	18
Burning - Caustic substances	9
Kicking/Stamping	31
Stabbing	58
Choking/Strangling/Suffocation	32
Illegal trapping/hunting	14
Throwing	69
Theft	27
Unlawful trade/Smuggling	14
Burning – Fire/Fireworks	95
Vehicular	85
Hoarding	250
Poisoning	70
Fighting	256
Shooting	364
Drowning	32
Beating	287
Mutilation/Torture	353
Neglect/Abandonment	921
Unclassified	91

SOME ANIMALS ARE BRED and used mainly for their muscle power. Horses, bison, cattle, llamas, donkeys, and more unusual animals may spend all their lives carrying loads, pulling ploughs or vehicles. In poor countries where medicine and resources for humans are scarce, care for animals is not often a high priority.

⬆ *Oxen pull a plough in India. Provided the harness is properly fitted, the oxen should suffer no ill effects from their work.*

IN HARNESS

Animals that pull ploughs through muddy fields, or drag a heavy load in a wagon, need a well-designed collar. Blisters and grazes from poorly-fitted collars easily become infected, killing thousands of animals each year. The SPCA in Goa, India, shows films to farmers about how to replace harmful old equipment with cheap, humane alternatives.

TUSK FORCE

Many places were cut off by the 2004 Indian Ocean tsunami. In Thailand, Plai Sudor the elephant helped out, lifting cars and moving rubble to search for bodies. Plai Sudor would have been "broken" to service painfully, taught to fear its handler. Thai campaigner Sangduen Chailert wants to change those training methods. She runs a sanctuary for elephants.

DIRT CHEAP DONKEYS

Most beasts of burden are valuable to their owner, but donkeys are cheap. In Israel, donkeys cost around £16 – less than the cost of a vet if they need medical attention. Many are abandoned when they become lame or old. The actor Anthony Head (Giles in *Buffy the Vampire Slayer*) became a sponsor to a donkey rescue charity there in 2004.

FACING THE ISSUES

The UK's Society for the Protection of ANimals Abroad (SPANA) sends emergency relief for animals, such as veterinary care, to regions in crisis. In 2004, it tried to care for around 130,000 "beasts of burden" in Iraq, where war threatened the welfare of economically important working animals. This not only helped the animals, but, in the words of UK politician Tony Banks, contributed to "the rebirth of the country".

⬇ *In some countries, owners may not care for their donkeys when they are ill – it is cheaper to buy a new one.*

FOOD ANIMALS

SOME ANIMALS ARE FARMED to be killed and eaten, and to provide us with eggs or milk. We also take animals from the wild for food. Cruelty can happen as a result of poor farming practice, or uncaring "mass production", unsafe transport, or careless slaughtering.

FACTORY FARMING

Production with less human effort makes food cheaper. Many people are upset by the lack of humane treatment for intensively-farmed food animals. For example, pigs are raised in huge, air-tight barns, with strict hygiene controls to protect them from diseases. Welfare groups ask meat and dairy consumers to pay extra, for the cost of more caring farming styles.

Hens kept in a battery. Some people choose to buy free range eggs and meat, where the chickens are kept in larger spaces.

WHAT DO YOU THINK?

In general, the animals we eat are well kept and, as a result of our care, have more comfortable and more secure lives than they would in the wild. How does this thought affect your attitude to eating meat?

- How do you feel about paying extra for meat from animals that have been reared in more spacious conditions?
- Do you ever find out how the meat you are given to eat is produced? Does it affect your decision to eat it?
- What do you consider the advantages and disadvantages of being a vegetarian?
- What do you think would happen if everyone became vegetarian?

LIVE EXPORTS

Compassion in World Farming (CiWF) campaign to end the export of live animals. They argue that it is less cruel to kill animals first, and transport them frozen. For 11 weeks in 2003, 57,000 Australian sheep were trapped on a ship which was refused permission to unload. Saudi Arabia suspected the sheep were infectious. The 51,000 survivors eventually had to be donated to Eritrea, Africa.

A **foie gras** *farmer uses a funnel to tip grain directly into the stomach of a goose, to fatten up its liver.*

Sheep can be sensitive to stress, such as overcrowding. As a result, live export may cause them to suffer.

CRUEL FOOD?

Some types of food seem to involve more cruelty to animals than others. In Israel in 2003, a court ruled against farmers who produce *foie gras* (pronounced "fwah-grah") from geese. Foie gras is the swollen liver of a goose, fattened-up by tipping large amounts of grain into their stomachs using a funnel. The court verdict required *foie gras* farming to end in 2005.

FOOD FROM THE WILD

Fishermen in Taiji, Japan, drive dolphins into shallow inlets, where they are killed for meat. Hunting wild animals like this is thought to be cruel by some people. But Western protestors are seen by locals as insulting their morals and intelligence. In 2004, one Taiji fisherman explained to a reporter: "They think Japanese people are coloured people, and that's why they think we are fools."

ESPECIALLY IN WEALTHY countries, animals used as pets do not suffer much deliberate cruelty. But lack of awareness of their needs, or just overfeeding, can cause other types of suffering. The pet industry can also take measures to prevent cruelty, for example, by breeding and selling animals responsibly.

↘ This abandoned cat is being cared for by an animal welfare officer. Before rehoming, he or she will be "altered" (neutered or spayed) to help prevent population growth.

⬆ The Rottweiler is one of several dog breeds whose tail is traditionally docked.

PEDIGREE PAIN?

Some pets are known as "pedigree" – they are bred to match a particular body shape or colour. In dogs, the official definition of around 50 breeds includes a "docked" tail, shortened to a stub. Some people feel that docking is cruel and want it banned. Sweden banned it in 1989, but found that hunting dogs with un-docked tails suffered frequent tail injuries.

POPULATION CONTROL

One of the biggest risks facing dogs and cats in wealthy countries is being abandoned. Excess supplies of kittens and puppies lead to many being killed without finding a home. Welfare groups work to help owners sterilize their pets, to prevent them breeding. In Singapore, for example, volunteers with the Cat Welfare Society help sterilize feral cats.

NO BARK, NO BITE

When dogs cause nuisance to neighbours by barking, some countries permit owners to have their vocal cords operated on. This makes their bark much quieter, and is called "de-barking". Those who favour de-barking for "talkative" dogs argue that the only alternative is more cruel – rejecting the dog. Opponents claim talkative dogs can be trained not to bark.

EXOTICS

The 2003 animated film *Finding Nemo* featured a striped, fishy character based on an Australian clownfish. Despite the expense and effort needed to care for a salt-water fish, sales of clownfish increased dramatically. Pets such as these are called "exotics". Animal welfare groups advise that they are suited to a specific environment, and should never be released elsewhere.

→ *In the wild, clownfish find safety amongst the stinging tentacles of a sea anemone. It is very difficult to recreate this habitat in a tank in the home.*

FACING THE ISSUES

Animal rights organizations such as PeTA argue that owning pets is an abuse of the animal's rights. PeTA claims that "more than 70 per cent of people who acquire animals end up giving them away, abandoning them, or taking them to shelters" in the USA. The British RSPCA does not oppose owning pets, but advises against keeping exotic animals such as large reptiles or salt-water tropical fish.

MOST CULTURES HAVE TRADITIONS

of using animals for entertainment, or sport. Animals may be put at risk of harm, in sports such as horse-racing, or deliberately killed in hunting or "blood sports". Limiting the use of animals for sport means banning some people's valued traditions. Strong emotions are raised on either side of the debate.

A hunt passes by a watching hunt saboteur dressed in army fatigues.

HUNTING, SHOOTING AND FISHING

In 2004, England and Wales banned the use of hounds to hunt mammals such as foxes. Foxhunting was practised by a few thousand traditional huntsmen and women, who saw it as a vital part of the fabric of rural community life. The Labour government promised it would not ban shooting and fishing – sports which involve millions of Britons.

DOMINO EFFECT?

Since April 2002, breeding pheasants for release as "game" birds has been illegal in the Netherlands. Previous laws allowed land owners to release birds to replace those lost to farming practices, such as nest damage during mowing. The Netherlands' example may help anti-hunting campaigners in Europe and elsewhere to campaign against organised "shoots".

DOG'S LIFE

Critics of dog racing want it banned because dogs are often treated inhumanely. They may be shot or abandoned when they are no longer fit to race, at just a few years of age. But retired racing greyhounds can also be adopted by families. Canada's Adopt-a-Greyhound.org website lists greyhound adoption agencies all around the world.

At a greyhound adoption centre in Connecticut, USA, a girl meets a retired dog, possibly her family's next pet.

RACING HOME

The American horse Seabiscuit, an "outsider" who became a champion in the 1930s, was still famous enough in 2003 to have a Hollywood film made about him. But racing can be dangerous for horses. The annual Grand National in the UK costs the lives of up to five horses each year. In 1997, New South Wales, Australia, banned this style of horse race.

GET THE FACTS STRAIGHT

This list shows the extent of hunting around Europe – and the amount of money spent on it. The statistics were gathered before the UK banned hunting with dogs.

Country	Number of hunters	Percentage of population	Hunters per square km	Annual spend on hunting in Euros
Belgium	29,000	0.29	0.81	235,500,000
Denmark	177,000	3.47	4.11	not available
Finland	300,000	5.96	0.89	173,000,000
France	1,650,000	2.89	3.00	1,950,100,000
Germany	338,000	0.42	0.95	736,300,000
Greece	293,000	2.84	2.22	not available
Ireland	120,000	3.43	1.71	63,500,000
Italy	925,000	1.62	3.07	not available
Netherlands	33,500	0.22	0.81	not available
Portugal	300,000	3.00	3.37	149,600,000
Spain	1,000,000	2.56	1.98	27,000,000
Sweden	320,000	3.64	0.71	174,000,000
UK	625,000	1.12	2.56	4,013,400,000

RELIGIOUS RITUALS *may involve animals, or completely forbid their use. Hinduism and Buddhism prefer vegetarianism, and Jainism requires veganism. But Judaism, Christianity and Islam all permit meat eating. No world religion makes meat eating compulsory. But some religious festivals, such as the Hajj and Turkey's Kurban Bayrami, traditionally require animals to be "sacrificed".*

RITUAL KILLING

The Jewish shechita and Islamic shariah laws describe similar methods to kill a food animal. The arteries of the neck are cut in one swift movement, to drain the blood and cause instant death. In 2003, a Jewish-run slaughterhouse in Postville, USA, was criticized by PeTA for failing to meet shechita standards. But Jewish and US government inspectors found nothing wrong.

DIVINE PIGS

The Hakkas people of the island of Taiwan hold an annual religious event at the Yimin Festival. Before the event, "divine pigs" are fattened to obesity. The fattest pig wins the competition to be the festival's main sacrifice. In 2003, animal rights activists accused Taiwanese president Chen Shui-bian of responsibility for the death of the 720kg "President Pig", sacrificed in his name.

Animal rights campaigners in France protest about the killing of sheep under Islamic shariah laws.

HIGH DAYS AND HOLIDAYS

Meals using special foods, such as turkey, goose or hare, may be a non-religious tradition linked with a religion. In 2002, animal rights group Dierenbescherming, in the Netherlands, placed advertisements with the Christian Virgin Mary cradling a dead, bleeding hare, to encourage Dutch Christians to end their tradition of eating a hare at Christmas.

ARTISTIC INSPIRATION

Some non-religious people use other aspects of human culture to replace religious experiences. The artist Marco Evaristti was briefly arrested in 2000 for a piece he installed in a Danish gallery, with live goldfish in 10 food blending machines. The artwork gave its audience the ability to choose whether to "blend" the live fish or not – making them grapple with their own morals.

⬇ Marco Evaristti's installation **Helena**. Would you turn on the blender?

WHAT DO YOU THINK?

⬆ A tranquilised rhinoceros after dehorning. It has been dehorned in an attempt to stop poachers killing it to sell its horn for TCM.

Tiger bones, rhinoceros horns and bear bile are all ingredients in traditional Chinese medicine (TCM). Poaching of these rare animals to supply a growing market is threatening extinction to many species. But millions of consumers want to purchase medicines according to their traditional ways of life, even if they put those species at risk. Do you think a trade like this should be banned without persuading TCM consumers to change their purchasing habits?

RESEARCH INTO ANIMALS *may just involve observation, such as Jane Goodall used, to study wild chimpanzees in the 1960s and 1970s. But animals are also used for biological and medical research in ways which harm them. They are used for tests and experiments that are too risky or harmful to be performed on a human volunteer. This form of experiment is known as vivisection.*

⊘ *A rabbit recovers from an operation performed on it in a medical experiment.*

LIVING BEINGS

Laboratory-bred rats, mice and other rodents make up around 85 per cent of all animals used in experiments, while specially-bred dogs and cats make up less than half of 1 per cent. Some campaigners argue that such research is not only cruel, but teaches us nothing relevant to human medicine, and even leads to dangerous drugs. The vast majority of scientists disagree.

THE THREE Rs

In 1959, the Universities Federation for Animal Welfare published advice for animal researchers known as the "three Rs": Reducing the number of animals used to a minimum; Refining how they are used, to minimise harm; Replacing animals where an alternative research method is available.

OTHER OPTIONS

In 2002, the EU launched a safety review of materials, such as plastics, in consumer goods. Thirty thousand materials needed testing. The European Centre for the Validation of Alternative Methods (ECVAM) studied which types of safety test could be run without animals. It found that the more complex risks, such as those from breathing in a material, still required animal testing.

TRANSPLANT TESTING

Some medical procedures are tried out first on animals, before being used for humans. Thomas Starzl pioneered liver and kidney transplants in the 1960s. He points out that, of the four test groups he used to perfect his technique, multiple deaths occurred only in the first three. These test groups were made up of dogs. The fourth group were humans.

This woman will be dependent on a dialysis machine for all her life unless she has a kidney transplant.

GET THE FACTS STRAIGHT

321,000 animals were used in experiments in New Zealand in 2003 for the following research aims:

Species conservation	1.8%
Environmental management	2.6%
Animal husbandry	3.7%
Basic biological research	36.2%
Medical research	12.5%
Veterinary research	14.8%
Commercial work	17.5%
Teaching	10.5%
Other	0.4%

In the UK in the same period 2,791,781 animals were involved in experiments for biological and medical research (of which 4 per cent were for safety tests on commercial products such as food additives).

ANIMALS AND EDUCATION

HUMANS USE ANIMALS to teach children and students a range of topics, from "life skills" and biology to sociology and medicine. Until quite recently in many countries, it was normal for biology students to learn anatomy by investigating the body of a dead rat or frog. This use of animals – called mortisection – is now usually optional for students.

↗ *Some girls perform a mortisection on a frog in a biology class.*

LEARNING EMOTION

Children's emotional development may be helped by owning a pet. Pets teach children how to be responsible for another living being, and prepare them to cope with harsh emotional challenges in their adult lives, such as bereavement. In 1999, Claudia Lamanna set up a support group in Ohio, USA, for adults who feel unable to cope with the death of a pet.

RABBIT FOOD

The cookery class at Ledgemont High School, USA, became notorious in 2005. A 16-year-old student, known as a keen hunter, was given permission to bring in a rabbit he had caught to prepare a meal. The student failed to hunt a rabbit, so he bought, killed and cooked a rabbit from a pet shop. Headlines about "pets cooked in class" forced the school to review its policies.

CLOSE ENCOUNTERS

TV programmes let children see animals in the wild. But the experience of being close to one – or even touching one – can stimulate more curiosity and understanding about animals. This is one of the benefits provided by zoos and aquariums. In Oita, Japan, the Marine Palace aquarium offers more than just viewing. It features basket-balling sea otters, puzzle-solving octopi and archer fish spitting at targets. Visitors are amazed at their skills and intelligence level.

LIFE-SAVERS

Military doctors have to deal with extreme wounds, caused by machine guns or flying fragments of metal, called "shrapnel". Medics train by sedating pigs or goats, and then wounding them with the relevant weapon. In September 2004, the Humane Society of the USA asked the Pentagon to replace goats with dummies for medical training at Fort Carson.

WHAT DO YOU THINK?

- Why do you think dissecting a dead animal could help your biology studies?
- How do you think vets should learn to perform operations?
- What educational benefits are there in visiting zoos or wildlife parks?
- What do you think of animals being "trained", in effect being forced to adopt human culture? Does the method of training make a difference?

⬇ *Most children enjoy a visit to the zoo and learn from it as well.*

25

WELFARE OR RIGHTS?

SOLUTIONS TO ANIMAL CRUELTY *take two main forms. The oldest, the animal welfare or "humane" approach, is seen by some as old fashioned. But it is widely supported, and prevents huge amounts of animal suffering. The more recent "animal rights" approach is more fashionable. It treats the human use of animals as slavery or even "genocide".*

HUMANE CARE

The idea of animal welfare flows from the belief that humans should never be cruel, or blind to suffering. It is concerned that we act "humanely" towards animals. Animal welfare groups care for tens of thousands of lost or injured animals around the world. This work appeals to older people. In 2005, cat-lover Betty Napier left $1 million in her will to the New Zealand SPCA.

The Nazis, notorious for their abuse of human rights, passed laws banning vivisection on animals. This cartoon shows animals saluting Hermann Goering, the Nazi behind the legislation.

Contrary to popular opinion, pigs are clean animals and enjoy washing in water. In January 2000, Denmark introduced laws requiring showers to be installed in pig sties.

FREE BY RIGHT

In the 1970s, a new wave of animal advocates argued that animal welfare was the wrong approach. Instead, we should recognise the "fact" that animals have rights, and treat any human use of animals as a type of slavery. Most animal rights campaigners believe that animals have rights, while vegetables do not, because animals suffer pain when harmed.

ANIMAL EXTREMISTS

For a few people, the scale of human "injustice" towards animals makes violence against humans acceptable. Graham Hall is an investigative TV journalist whose programme, *Inside the ALF*, showed Animal Liberation Front activists discussing bomb-making. After his exposé, he was kidnapped by masked men, beaten, and had the letters ALF burned onto his back with a hot iron. Laboratories where vivisection takes place now have to spend large sums of money on security measures for their staff – money that could be spent on medical research – for fear of violent attack from animal rights activists.

➡ *Some animal rights activists believe in taking direct action – removing dogs from laboratories for example.*

Many animal welfare groups support the idea of "five freedoms" to ensure the welfare of farm and pet animals:

- Freedom from hunger, thirst and malnutrition
- Freedom from physical and thermal discomfort
- Freedom from pain, injury, and disease
- Freedom to express normal behaviour
- Freedom from fear and distress.

THE HUMAN RELATIONSHIP *to animals has reached a fork in the road. In one direction, welfare laws will slowly change how animals are treated. Farm animals, pets, laboratory animals and others will be increasingly protected. In the other direction, aspects of that relationship will be banned outright – and animal rights activists will continue to agitate to bring about still greater changes in attitude.*

⬇ *This US PeTA campaign promotes both animal rights and Christianity. The group often takes controversial steps to obtain publicity.*

FAIR TRADE

Better farm animal welfare in wealthy countries forces importers from developing countries to meet tougher standards. Some poor countries see this as an excuse for wealthy countries to protect their farmers from competition. China joined the World Trade Organization in 2001. With India, Brazil, and other developing countries, it will try to lower such barriers to trade.

BAD OLD DAYS

Traditional cultural practices are becoming harder to defend, especially when a minority engage in them, or when their main purpose appears to be entertainment. Sports which involve killing or hurting animals, from hunting to bullfighting, are being closed down across Europe and the world. Animals in circuses, and eventually zoos, may soon be phased out.

Members of SHAC gather together to protest against Huntingdon Life Science.

The UK campaign to Stop Huntingdon Animal Cruelty (SHAC) focused on closing one animal research firm, Huntingdon Life Sciences (HLS). The campaign threatened employees of any company doing business with HLS. Non-violent threats turned into violence when three SHAC supporters attacked the firm's manager with pickaxe handles. This new type of campaigning spread to America. Patti Strand, of an anti-animal rights organization there, said: "We view the United Kingdom as the Afghanistan for the growth of animal rights extremism throughout the world. The animal rights movement that we are dealing with in the United States is a direct import from the United Kingdom."

SECURITY COSTS

In the meantime, animal rights activists will continue to promote their cause – through publicity stunts and more extreme action, such as that of SHAC (see panel). The cost of medical research using animals will rise, as companies and universities pay to secure their buildings and staff from animal rights activists. The UK scientists' organization, the Royal Society, found in 2004 that the extra cost per university was already £175,000 each year. Governments are likely to become involved, partly as they risk losing scientists to countries with less animal rights activism.

NEW AUTHORITARIANISM

Governments are responsible for maintaining law and order and how they do this is constantly under review. On the one side, they have to deal with animal rights extremism. On the other, when they pass laws banning animal uses, minorities such as hunters may mount unlawful protests. Both challenges to law and order will prove hard to contain using traditional policing. Instead, governments will explore new controls on protest and free movement, which are more authoritarian and may create new risks for democracy.

GLOSSARY

abattoir: A slaughterhouse; hygienic space where food animals are sent to be killed.

authoritarian: Where authority (usually the government and the people who enforce its laws) is more important than freedom of the individual.

baiting: Setting an animal (for example a dog) onto a captive animal (such as a bear or badger) for entertainment.

cultural: To do with human arts, crafts, traditions, rituals and ways of life.

docking: Removing between one half and two thirds of a puppy's tail, at around three days old.

feral: Describes animals that were formerly domesticated but have returned to the wild.

foie gras: Fattened goose or duck liver, produced by forced feeding of the live animal.

Hajj: Annual pilgrimage to Mecca, Saudi Arabia, every Muslim should try to complete once in his or her lifetime.

humane: Merciful, kind, opposed to suffering.

intensive farming: Raising animals indoors, scientifically, to produce meat or dairy products more efficiently and more cheaply.

live export: Moving livestock to a foreign customer while it is still alive.

matador: Qualified bullfighter, fighting alone and on foot, with cape and sword.

moral: A rule or idea for living decently with other people, such as "be caring".

pet industry: The businesses related to keeping pets, such as animal breeders, pet shops, manufacturers of pet food, accessories and medicines.

PeTA: People for the Ethical Treatment of Animals, the best-funded animal rights group in the world.

poacher: A person who hunts animals or fish illegally.

rights: A special type of moral, legal or political claim, superior to all other laws.

sadism: being deliberately cruel, particularly where pain is inflicted, and deriving pleasure from the act.

sanctuary: Safe area for people or animals at risk of harm.

soul: In religions, the thinking and feeling part of a human, distinct from the physical body. Some people believe animals also have souls.

veganism: Against the use of animal products, for example meat, leather, honey and dairy products. A vegan diet is a strict form of vegetarianism where no animal products are included.

vegetarian: Diet excluding meat and fish. It can include dairy products, such as milk, cheese and eggs.

vivisection: Making surgical operations on living animals for the purpose of scientific research.

warden: Official protecting a park or animals from poachers.

welfare: Well-being, access to the necessities of life.

The websites listed here will help you look further into the issues surrounding cruelty to animals. This list excludes organizations that promote or support illegal activities.

altweb.jhsph.edu
Alternatives to animal experiments – a balanced view. See the educational resources frequently asked questions.

www.animalsaustralia.org
Aims to bring together different animal rights and welfare groups who campaign on similiar issues. Also has links with New Zealand groups.

www.armyths.org
A "Frequently Asked Questions" page critical of "facts" used in animal rights propaganda.

www.bret.org.uk
Biomedical Research Education Trust, information resource in defence of vivisection.

www.cdb.org/defra/sub1.htm
The Council of Docked Breeds (UK) makes a welfare argument for continuing to dock dogs' tails.

www.elephantnaturepark.org
Thailand's elephant rescue charity and "Elephant Heaven" sanctuary.

www.goaspca.org
Goa Society for the Prevention of Cruelty to Animals.

www.ibrrc.org
International Bird Rescue Research Center – news on oil spills and other rescue operations.

www.janegoodall.org
Institute set up by the world-famous chimpanzee scientist to improve welfare for primates.

www.kids4research.org
American animal experimentation advocates present information designed for school students.

usda.mannlib.cornell.edu/
A database of farming statistics in the USA.

www.mundo-taurino.org
English language site linking to pro- and anti- bullfighting resources on the web.

www.naiaonline.org
US-based resource for animal welfare supporters, opposed to animal rights activism.

www.petakids.com
Children's site for the People for the Ethical Treatment of Animals. The biggest animal rights group.

www.rivercottage.net/ foodmatters
UK TV chef Hugh Fearnley-Whittingstall comments about food matters, including his "meat manifesto".

www.rspca.org.uk
www.rspca.org.au
The Royal Society for the Prevention of Cruelty to Animals. The oldest animal welfare society in the world. Operates in the UK and Australia.

www.safehaven4donkeys.org
Donkey rescue charity working in Israel and Palestine.

www.vare.org.uk
Victims of Animal Rights Extremism, a support group for people targeted by animal rights activists.

www.vivisection-absurd.org.uk
Animal rights advocacy site putting the case against animal experimentation.